10 Truths to Transform Your Team into Winners

Michael Duke

Harrods Creek Publishing
Louisville, Kentucky 2006

Coach to the Goal: 10 Truths to Transform Your Team into Winners
Copyright © 2006 by Michael Duke. All rights reserved.

ISBN-13 978-1-60145-113-2
ISBN-10 1-60145-113-X

Published in association with Jeff P. Emerson, Editorial Advisor, Goshen, Kentucky.

All rights reserved. No part of this publication may be reproduced, stored in a retrieval system, or transmitted in any form or by any means — electronic, mechanical, photocopy, recording or any other — except for brief quotations in printed reviews, without the prior permission of the publisher.

To Winfred and Miriam Duke

Your love and devotion as parents can only be matched by your love and devotion to each other.

I love you.

"Coach to the Goal will change your perspective from focusing on the daily tasks to focusing on, and having a genuine concern for, your employees. To see your role as a "Coach" will change your thinking and help you build a motivated team atmosphere in your business. I've read a lot of leadership books, but *Coach to the Goal* has really challenged me to view my role as a leader in a different way that will make me more effective."

David Stewart
CEO International Moulding Co.

"If people are important to your business, then you need to read this book! You will wish you had learned this information years earlier! *Coach to the Goal* is an engaging, easy read with valuable insights into the people part of your business."

David Jarnagin
CEO Coolbakers International

"Michael's ideas on coaching have become part of our manager's 'basic training.' The core message of *Coach to the Goal* – honest, timely, caring and clear communication about our competitive needs – is essential to our future success!"

Robert DeAngelis
Vice President, Louisville Tile Distributors

"Coaches are driven to help other people win. They love to succeed and understand that they don't prevail on their own. But rather, they're victorious through others."

– Michael Duke

Contents

INTRODUCTION 1

PART ONE: THE POWER OF THE COACHING PHILOSOPHY 6

Truth No. 1 – Value the Heart of Your Players 6

Truth No. 2 – Build Your Team on Values 13

Truth No. 3 – You Win When Your People Win 23

PART TWO: THE POWER OF THE CONSEQUENCE . 33

Truth No. 4 – Earn the Right to Coach Everyday 33

Truth No. 5 – Clear, Consistent Accountability 38

Truth No. 6 – Their Attitude Reflects Your Leadership 45

Truth No. 7 – Be a Teacher 50

PART THREE: THE POWER OF PRAISE 59

Truth No. 8 – No One Is There Yet 59

Truth No. 9 – Love Them or Trade Them 74

Truth No. 10 – Treat Them As if They Were "More Than" 80

CONCLUSION 95

ACKNOWLEDGEMENTS 99

RECOMMENDED READING ON THE SUBJECT OF COACHING 101

MICHAEL'S TOP 10 102

ABOUT THE AUTHOR 105

SHARE IT WITH OTHERS 107

HOW TO INVITE MICHAEL TO SPEAK 108

Introduction

The philosophy presented in *Coach to the Goal* is not new. But as a reader, you'll be asked to view familiar situations in a new and different way. And if you're a leader, my goal is to challenge you to ask yourself, "Why am I here? What is my preeminent responsibility as a leader, manager or supervisor?" My hope is that you'll learn your role is to make a positive impact on people who are under your influence. The lens of a coach may help you see this more clearly.

And when you go home each day and ask yourself was today well-spent and did I do good, you will answer yes only when you have looked into the eyes of your people and with words that are strong, clear and compassionate somehow make them better than they were that morning. The growth may be barely noticeable to the naked eye.

But as their coach, you will notice and they will know that you know. The players on your team long for a leader who will teach; challenge; and love them right where they are.

Michael Duke

As you become a coach, you'll learn what winning really means. You'll begin to keep score differently. And the journey of success will mean more than its attainment.

You'll see more value in people than results and focus more on opportunities than failures. The faces will stand out over forms.

That which is excellent – but yet cannot be quantified – is the coach's source of strength. Personal, emotional, mental and spiritual growth is the path toward victory – no matter what the scoreboard says. Why? True victory, which is sustainable over time, is not measured in an afternoon or a day but rather in a lifetime.

All the great coaches knew that it was never about *the* game. It has been and always will be about the players and making them great.

Coach to the Goal

Great players have always found great coaches. It will always be this way. Those who are so fortunate as to grasp this elusive truth change the world together. Coach John Wooden got it. He and his UCLA Bruins altered the face of men's college basketball. It will never be the same.

Coach Wooden "Coached to the Goal," as sure as any man alive ever has. And what did he accomplish? He was named the Coach of the Century.

Because of Herb Kelleher and his Southwest Team, the airline industry is forever changed. Unlike the other guys, Southwest hasn't experienced layoffs, cutbacks, strikes or bankruptcies. And they make more money. Why? Coach Kelleher "Coaches to the Goal."

He lives by the mantra: Put your people first and they'll love your customers and treat them like family.

Michael Duke

The way to successfully impact the win/loss column is not a direct attack. Focus on winning. Talk about winning and you lose. You win when your people win. And they win when they're taught to pursue and attain personal excellence in all they do.

They leave the team at some point and because you were their coach, they now know more about sacrifice, honor, effort, sportsmanship, integrity, love and life. How can they not win wherever they go? They are already winners. You taught them more than a game. You taught them how to live well and lose well with pride and honor.

I am excited that you want to learn to "Coach to the Goal" I am honored that you have picked up this book. The words on every page are from my heart and represent half a lifetime of lessons learned. I believe that leaders who coach are the most effective leaders of all. Why?

You find them "leading with the heart," which by the way is the title of Coach K's (Mike Krzyzewski, coach of the Duke University men's basketball team) book on leadership.

I love to coach and learn. I challenge you to open up your heart and mind and push back on every page." Teach me by sending me your thoughts to **mduke@michaelduke.com**. I look forward to hearing from you, as you learn to *Coach to the Goal*.

Part One: The Power of the Coaching Philosophy

Truth No. 1 – Value the Heart of Your Players

Great coaches love their players. It is absolutely inherent. You can be an average or above-average coach; however, you've got to love your people to be an excellent one. You love your people by living out of a desire to help them learn and grow. Coaches are all about their players and not themselves.

Coaches are driven to help other people win. They love to succeed and understand that they don't prevail on their own. But rather, they're victorious through others. So when you're looking to advance someone into a leadership role, first ask yourself: "Do they win independently or do they work and play well with others?" "Do they really have the love and passion to help others grow?" These questions are critical in the coaching philosophy.

Let me demonstrate using this scenario:

The worst mistake often made in a sales environment is when the wrong person is selected for a sales manager position. You might imagine the most qualified person for this role would be a salesperson whose numbers are consistently the highest. Despite the success, a top-performing salesperson is typically driven by his or her needs and goals and not by an innate desire to help others. Therefore, the best salesperson on the team may not be the best fit for promotion to sales manager.

The best leader may be the sales person who performs in the middle of the pack, yet takes time on their own to assist the rookies and the struggling. When they help others without being asked, their true heart is revealed. Every leader and every team needs a heart.

Your role as a coach is to transform the lives of the people around you. Coaches teach and motivate – all in their own style. This book provides a leadership philosophy that's different from what so many others are used to.

Intelligent coaches recognize raw potential in people – such as good eye-hand coordination and speed – and they nurture it into something extraordinary.

And though it doesn't take any particular skill, a player must possess heart and character to drive his or her own destiny. The coach is merely a guide, a mentor—a special individual who can help the player achieve his or her capabilities.

I've recruited talent for my clients for more than 20 years. Most candidates look like the perfect hire because their résumés present textbook skills and qualifications. Yet many have neither shown me the passion nor drive that's necessary to reach greatness. I'll take a person with heart and character any day over the perfect résumé.

In Jim Collins' book, *Good to Great*, he talks about placing people on the bus and putting them in the right seats. It's my intention to fill the bus with great people, and work with them so they're in the right positions. But first, you must examine their heart and character.

Without these qualities, skill and experience alone are worthless to an employer. How many organizations do you know focus on heart and character in its selection process?

Legendary NFL coach Vince Lombardi, who guided the Green Bay Packers to six division titles, five championships and two Super Bowls (I and II), amassed a 98-30-4 record in nine seasons. He said, "It is essential to understand that battles are primarily won in the hearts of men."

What's interesting is that Lombardi knew about getting the right people on the team and moving them into the right positions later. For example, after making Herb Adderley the Packers' first draft choice in 1961 (12th overall), Lombardi and the coaching staff tried him in a variety of positions on offense.

In the book *Run to Daylight*, Lombardi wrote: "I had been so stubborn trying to make him (Adderley) something that he didn't want to be – a flanker. He wanted to be a defensive back." As it turns out, Adderley had the intelligence, speed and instinct to make the switch. His training as a receiver and rusher at Michigan State University transferred readily to the defensive side of the ball. And his sure hands and speed made him a threat as a kick returner.

Bound for the Hall of Fame, Adderley became an All-Pro only after Lombardi agreed to move him to defense. Adderley was good as an offensive player, but became great when moved to defense. This was a small, but significant coaching move. Great coaches, like Lombardi, look at the intangibles.

They have the innate ability to make little changes that yield significant results. Do you evaluate your players in such a manner? Can you look deep enough within them to see something that may help you move them to greatness?

> *"Unless a man believes in himself and makes a total commitment to his career and puts everything he has into it – his mind, his body and his heart – what's life worth to him?"*
>
> **- Coach Lombardi**

Michael Duke

It's so easy to judge people by their performance. For example, if a student has a C-minus or D grade-point average, society perceives him or her as an underachiever. It's impossible to evaluate someone by a report card, by how they look, or by how well they perform on a particular job. It may be the easy way out, but one must not fall prey to this behavior. The fact is many famous people, who we consider geniuses because of their accomplishments, were not outstanding students or prodigies at all. To the closed mind, they just did not fit the traditional mold of what excellence looks like.

Do you know that some of the greatest sports movies are based on this truth? In the movie *"Rudy,"* for example, a young man was always told he was too small to play college football. But his determination to overcome the odds and fulfill his dream of playing for the University of Notre Dame was simply awe-inspiring.

I'll take four or five players like Rudy on my team any day because they have what it takes to become winners. Heart, desire, passion, discipline, intelligence and character are worth more than all the skill in the world.

As a coach in business, it's your responsibility to build a world-class organization. You have your own style, but it's time to think outside the box by breaking customary recruiting habits and focusing on a potential candidate's character and heart – you'll be glad you did.

Michael Duke

Truth No. 2 – Build Your Team on Values

Skills, degrees and experiences are all important and should be carefully reviewed. However, it's equally imperative to look into a candidate's character and values, from which flow the drive and determination required for personal and organizational growth.

Southwest Airlines' business model doesn't fit the "normal" mold you'd find at other organizations. Herb Kelleher, Southwest's co-founder and executive chairman, said in an interview that the Southwest model has been written about in textbooks for the past 10 to 15 years.

Southwest is a huge airline, which has never had a layoff. Its retention rate is over 90 percent and people are waiting in line to get a job.

But you know what's so interesting? Unless you're a pilot or mechanic, no airline experience is required at Southwest. That's right! Airline experience will not help you to get a job there. In fact, it could potentially turn out to be a negative.

The Southwest selection model is set up to identify people who will thrive in the airline's unique culture. The person who fits well within the Southwest culture will have their own personal blend of personality, heart and people-orientation. People love to work at Southwest because the company hires for character and trains for skill.

Now let's refer to Kenneth Blanchard's book, *The One Minute Manager,* where he says, "Everyone is a potential winner. Some people are simply disguised as losers." Think for a minute about the different kinds of people you work with who may qualify as losers.

They might not perform well, or they may have a bad attitude. And then there are the folks who execute their jobs quite well.

So what's wrong with this picture?

Repeat aloud, "Everyone is a potential winner." Blanchard shows us an important truth—a powerful affirmation that personifies the character and attitude all coaches need. It's your job to figure out how to make your people winners. It's important that we stop blaming player performance and start looking at player value.

Coaches who build effective teams that sustain success over time develop each team member first. How serious are *you* taking this responsibility? Are your people in the right role? Whose job is it to get them in the right place? Are you doing your job as a coach? Are you committed to making each player the best they can be?

> *"Make your values visible to let the outside world know – potential employees and others – what you stand for and who you are. In doing so, you will attract others who share similar principles and standards – your code of conduct for competition."*
>
> **- Coach John Wooden**

Most business owners or executives I've coached have "Type A" personalities. They spend most of their time accomplishing tasks. And because they're so task-oriented, they often forget about their employees by not giving them the attention they deserve. This typically has a negative impact.

And like business owners, coaches have different communication styles. Bobby Knight (also known as the General) is the men's head basketball coach at Texas Tech University. Knight's fiery temper is well known and his on-court antics are the stuff of a legend. But let me say this, Knight seems to know how to win by instilling discipline and team work.

One of the quietest, most effective NFL coaches was Tom Landry. He led the Dallas Cowboys to two Super Bowl titles (1972, '78), five NFC titles, and 13 divisional titles while compiling a 270-178-6 record – the third most all-time victories for a NFL coach.

Landry was the type of coach who generally didn't give a half-time speech. He left that to his assistant coaches. "We just prepare the guys. They are men," Landry said. "They know what we need them to do. Come game day, I expect them to do what they have been trained to do."

Rick Pitino is now the University of Louisville men's basketball coach. When Pitino first came to U of L, he did something I thought was quite unique. Pitino's teams are well-known for their discipline and physical stamina, and they've earned a reputation for outlasting their opponents.

When Pitino first met with the U of L squad, he said: "I keep myself fit. I personally keep a disciplined regimen and all my players and coaches will be fit." Pitino set a standard. A coach or two had a decision to make. Do I lose the weight or my job? All stayed and the standard inspired the entire team, coaches and players alike.

Pitino's players and peers respect him because he applies the same rules across the board for everyone.

Michael Duke

You inspire people with your actions, not by your words alone.

Now I'd like for you to close your eyes and think about your favorite teacher. Picture them and pause for a moment. Do you have a name? Do you remember the subject(s) they taught? Ask yourself why you picked this person? Were they your easiest teacher allowing you to get away with everything? Perhaps they were just plain fun.

Actually, most people remember the teachers who were demanding but fair. Personally, my favorite teachers inspired me because they weren't pushovers. They challenged and inspired me to be more. I learned a lot from them about life and about myself. Perhaps it was due to my discipline, or that I had a passion about the subject. Regardless, they planted the seeds for my future. And that's what good coaches are supposed to do.

Coaches touch people's lives forever because they know how to invest in people in order to reach their maximum potential. Whether it's one-on-one or in groups, I love coaching and I'm trying to make a difference. I love to learn truths and apply them to my life while sharing them with others. How can you teach others if you're not always learning as well?

When I was working in the corporate environment for a publisher and advertiser, my team had developed a great strategic plan. Corporate had blessed it. We were executing it well.

But one day, I had received a phone call from my vice president saying, "We just learned that we have a copyright in the Michigan market and if we don't use it pretty soon, we may lose the rights to it."

While I didn't fully comprehend all the legal aspects, nothing else mattered when my vice president said, "We have got to figure out a way to use this thing immediately." So, every plan we had previously implemented was dumped in order to create the latest plan for a new magazine title.

All of our ongoing initiatives were placed on the back burner. We diverted our attention to this new title introduction. It went well. But we sacrificed important time and energy designed to develop and grow our team to a project that no one claimed would move our business forward.

This was nothing but reactionary and short term. The focus was on the present. There wasn't really any long-term plan and any fluctuations were not tolerated—yet this is so unrealistic.

The United States of America is the greatest country in the world. But many businesses in America operate on short-term fixes instead of keeping a keen eye on long-term goals. Did you know that Japanese organizations develop 50-year strategic plans? Can you imagine creating such a plan and sticking to it?

Truth No. 3 – *You Win When Your People Win*

To borrow a quote from Blanchard, "The most important minute you spend every day is what? The one you invest in people. That's the most important minute."

I'm not saying that revenues, expenses, quarterly goals and corporate objectives are unimportant. Please don't misunderstand me. Rather, they're not *the* most important things. The bottom line is that we must foster relationships with people to help them get tasks done more effectively.

Excellence sustained over time as expressed in revenues, income and market share results from the successful design and implementation of your people development process. If your people win, you will too!

Michael Duke

How you treat your employees is important. Look at what happened with Enron. Many people held Enron, which was once the nation's seventh-largest company, responsible for one of the biggest business scandals in U.S. history. It wasn't the company that was at fault.

Instead, it was Enron's two former chiefs who were convicted of conspiracy and securities and wire fraud. Many of Enron's employees trusted their leaders and lost everything. While we tend to believe companies fail us, it's the leaders who fall short. Enron's strategy was neither long term nor people focused.

> *"You can't coach the <u>real</u> goal and react every day to your environment. If you're truly going to coach the <u>right</u> goal, you must provide your people with the appropriate time, training and communication. Since we'll always have environmental or external changes, the only way to win in the long term is to stay focused on your people."*
>
> **- Michael Duke**

> *"Each member of the team has the potential for personal greatness. The leader's job is to help them achieve it."*
>
> **- Coach Wooden**

Michael Duke

Are you getting the picture now? As you help others succeed, you're giving yourself – and the ones around you – an opportunity to accomplish great things. Years ago, renowned motivational speaker Zig Ziglar walked away from a record-setting sales career to help other people become more successful in their personal and professional lives.

Ziglar wrote, "It is my conviction that ambition, fueled by compassion, wisdom, and integrity, is a powerful force for good. It will turn the wheels of industry and open the door of opportunity for you and countless thousands of other people."

In the early 1980s I had listened to Ziglar at a positive, mental attitude rally. One of his quotes that really got my attention was: "He climbs highest who helps another up."

No matter what your calling – a pastor, an entrepreneur, a staff leader or most especially a coach – you can appreciate those words of wisdom. If we are to excel in leadership, we *must* help others succeed.

Numerous books were written in the early '70s and '80s, including Michael Korda's *Power,* which had described how to get ahead in business at all cost. The common theme was that you had to "be tougher than the other guy." It also said you had to have a "bust-some-heads" attitude. As we know today, these are words of deception.

The best book I've recently read is Tim Sanders' *Love Is the Killer App: How to Win Business and Influence Friends*. I highly recommend it.

Sanders contends that you must give your network (contacts) away. Share your knowledge for free at every opportunity and, most importantly, share your love. People appreciate kindness, courtesy and generosity. It will all come back to you in the end. Believe it.

Author Bob Moawad says, "Help others get ahead, and you will always stand taller with someone else on your shoulders." This is a good admonition for us all.

While I can be a demanding coach, who likes to win, I'm also a firm believer in what some refer to as the softer skills. Yes, I could be tough while working in corporate management, but I quickly learned that I couldn't win on my own. So no matter who you are, it takes a team to get you where you want to go.

As we talk about the coaching philosophy, let me remind you not to blame people. If your people can't perform, you've got to implement a process that measures and evaluates them at every opportunity. But if they can't cut it, look at yourself first.

It's no accident that turnover is higher and performance is lower with only certain coaches. The fault lies either in the quality of the recruit or the quality of the coach's program. And the coach controls both.

You may ask yourself, "Why am I bringing people onboard who can't cut it?" "I want to know what I'm doing that keeps my people from developing as well as they should." You'll probably find the answer once you start understanding differently.

And if you're not making a positive impact on people, you may need to reconsider what you as a coach are doing. Is your program effective? Does it value both people and performance?

Sometimes you may need to drop back and punt and re-evaluate your coaching goals. Let's talk about the Lombardi teams of the early 1960s. The Green Packers recorded a dismal 1-10-1 record in '59.

The following season, Lombardi was named head coach of the Packers and miraculously guided the squad into the championship game but to no avail. However, it was the turning point for the team and organization because the Packers went on to win three consecutive NFL championships ('61, '62 and '63) under Lombardi's reign.

Ironically, 13 players from the losing '59 team went on to become All Pro. What happened? Remember what I had mentioned earlier that everyone is a winner, but can be disguised as losers. That's what occurred here. There were 13 individuals who were *not* recognized as All-Pro players before their winning performances because people had focused solely on the win-loss column.

But Lombardi came along and saw winners. His coaching excellence propelled his players to the top, showing them how to become winners in the face of defeat. That's what great coaches do.

I'm not saying he was a perfect man, but he did some extraordinary things with the same core group of men from the '59 team. He taught them to believe first in himself as a coach and in his program.

Then he taught them to believe in themselves and the team. That's what Lombardi did. He made a difference in the lives of these men and became a legend while doing so.

Think about the people you influence in your life. What are you teaching them? Are you making a difference? Sometimes we make positive changes, sometimes negative ones. I've experienced both in my life.

But I ask you to stop and think about your people when you need to make changes. It might be easy to replace them when times are bad; however, it's not always the most effective course of action.

Consider keeping your employees or players and learn where they fit in the best.

Try to look past the misperceptions they may have earned and unveil the true winners in all your people. By doing so, you will have taken your first critical step toward *Coaching to the Goal*.

Recapping the Three Truths from Part One:

1. **Value the Heart of Your Players.** Skill is overrated. Heart and passion is the source of excellence and personal greatness. Coaches look for heart, nurture it and build the team on it.

2. **Build Your Team on Values.** Character and values lay the foundation for success. These virtues joined with skill are an unbeatable combination. Skill can be taught and enhanced. Character and values cannot.

3. **You Win When Your People Win.** Victory is not found in a score but in a life. Coaches never get lost in the game, but take the opportunity to make a difference by teaching others how to be excellent in every aspect of their life.

Part Two: The Power of the Consequence

Truth No. 4 – Earn the Right to Coach Everyday

Now that we've set the foundation for the philosophy of coaching, let's talk about the Power of Consequence, which tests our fear of confrontation and challenges us to apply consequences in the lives of others.

Here are three steps to keep you on your game as a coach. Follow them and you'll be ready for success:

1. **Coach's Preparation**
2. **Player Performance**
3. **Appropriate Consequences**

Coach's preparation begins with things as simple as setting agendas and being on time for meetings. There's nothing worse than arriving late for a meeting or being ill-prepared.

For example, I remember receiving a phone call from a friend. She was an advertising sales rep for a local radio station. She said to me, "The entire sales team and I are sitting here right now and the meeting was supposed to start 2½ hours ago. The manager is in their office on the phone and we're all in here waiting for him to get off and meet with us."

This makes people angry, frustrated and resentful.

You respect your people by respecting their time.

But let's look at the bigger picture. If you don't have character, you shouldn't be involved in a coaching role anyway. Great coaches come personally prepared, and they understand there are certain things they've got to do before they ask someone else to do something. One of them is earning the right to speak.

Whether you're the boss or the dad, you've got to earn the right to speak. I've learned this throughout my life. Have you ever heard yourself exclaiming, "I am the boss? Do what I say!" Or, "I am the dad. Do what I say!" I've stated these commands myself too many times and they don't work. Trust me!

You must *become* the kind of man or woman people respect. This is the most important aspect of the coach's preparation. When your players see you as prepared you earn the right to speak because you're respecting other people and gaining their respect simultaneously.

Player Performance is the way our people act or react to our leadership and instruction. This includes their attitude and their behavior. When coaching leaders, I often get the questions: "How do you confront someone about their attitude?"

"How do you tell them what attitude you want?" I agree. It seems hard to pinpoint, but you tell them what the right attitude looks like. Describe it to them.

Sometimes people don't know what the right thing is. But most people can identify the wrong things. Therefore, you must eliminate the negatives in order to get to the positives. You've got to help people with that.

Player Performance is what your employee brings to the table. And the **Appropriate Consequences** are what the coach delivers after a goal has either been accomplished or attempted. The important words are *attempted* or *accomplished*. Either way, there must be an appropriate consequence from the coach.

The better a coach is at his or her personal "preparation" and the more clearly and consistently they deliver "consequences," the better the employee will become at achieving "performance." When followed correctly these three steps will form an outstanding coaching strategy.

If your boss always arrives for work before you do and leaves after you do, he or she demonstrates a good work ethic and common business sense – both of which earn your respect.

On the other hand, if your boss arrives to work late, takes long lunches and leaves early, your opinion of them isn't very high is it? Your "coach preparation" behaviors build up a fund of goodwill with your team from which you may draw in the future, as you ask more of your players in the way of "player performance."

A poorly "prepared" coach has little or no power fund from which to draw. When he or she still asks for more "performance" from their players, they do not respond and the coach wonders what's wrong.

Is this a coaching problem or a player problem? You decide.

> *"My goal is to be worthy of the team's commitment."*
>
> **- Coach K**

Michael Duke

Truth No. 5 – Clear, Consistent Accountability

Consequences can be either negative or positive, but they must be appropriate. And as a leader they must be delivered in a timely manner. Studies have shown that 75 percent to 80 percent of influence on human behavior stems from consequences.

Well-known psychologist B.F. Skinner (1904-1990) said, "Behavior is followed by a consequence, and the nature of the consequence modifies the organism's tendency to repeat the behavior in the future." Remember Skinner's experiment with a mouse—the one that accidentally pushed a lever, which released a food pellet. The mouse continued to push the lever in order to receive the reward. The consequence (food pellet) caused a learned behavior.

Interestingly, many of us train people to do things for us and reward them for it. Some of us are more obvious than others. Are we rewarding the right behaviors or the wrong ones?

Be careful what you reward. Often, we reward deception and laziness. And sometimes you'll find that incentive programs are grossly inadequate. The most obvious one is when business owners are frustrated over not making enough profits.

Many companies pay salespeople based on top-line revenues. But why do businesses pay their salespeople on revenues when they want them to think profits?

If profits are the goal and they are for most companies then I contend that everyone must be focused on profits. That's why it's wise to build them into their incentives. Jack Welch, former General Electric chairman and CEO, said in his book, *Straight from the Gut*, that for people's behavior to change, you have to consistently make it a part of their compensation.

Consequences are not just talking to your people. Understand there are rewards and punishments. Some people exclaim, "Oh no, punishments! I'm not a child."

I don't care what word you're comfortable using. Just recognize when people do good things, they should be rewarded for it. This reward in essence "freezes" the good behaviors and increases the likelihood that it will continue.

When they perform certain behaviors that are unacceptable, you must discourage these behaviors with disciplinary action. A bad behavior quickly discouraged by an appropriately negative consequence will disappear. A bad behavior ignored will continue and ultimately fester.

As a coach, it's your job to implement consequences. Not because you want to or because it's easy, but because it's a necessary part of making people great.

Constructive feedback needs to be a part of your coaching program. Great coaches understand that successful relationships with team members require regular communication. Individually and as a team the coach needs to inform them of their progress.

In 2005, I was able to attend the Coach K Leadership Conference at Duke University. The highlight for all of us attending was to observe an entire Duke men's basketball practice at Cameron Indoor Stadium.

Coach K blew his whistle to stop practice often to tell his players what they were doing well and also what they needed to improve. He took the time to explain and even show them what the behavior he desired looked like.

Consequences may be difficult for many coaches to administer face to face, but as you make constructive feedback a part of your program, it'll get easier. It's very rare that people are doing everything poorly. So you're always going to have a worthwhile discussion about what they're doing well and what they can improve on next time.

If you don't use constructive feedback, it can be detrimental to the workplace and to relationships. I understand you might be too busy or may not feel well, but you must take the time to listen and respond.

Michael Duke

You say to yourself, "Why aren't my employees doing more or working harder?" More than likely, it's because you're not giving them constructive feedback. You've got to respond to your employees in a meaningful way or they'll become stagnant in their positions.

Kids don't do well without responses either. A friend of mine recently adopted a little girl who had spent the first five years of her life in an orphanage in Eastern Europe. The girl received food, had her diapers changed but wasn't cuddled or held enough. And now she's developmentally challenged. Your lack of attention given to your players can cause them to be developmentally challenged as well.

In my experience a great pitfall for many coaches is to neglect people and their performance. This lack of action is one that comes naturally to many. This fascinates me. If I have heard one leader, I have heard a hundred defend their lack of response to employees. They explain that they are just too busy to offer praise for genuine praiseworthy behavior.

If you, as a coach, are too busy to praise a great tackle, a great basket or a great sale, then you are too busy to be a coach.

And you would think it would be easier to praise the big things, but it's more challenging and more motivating to praise the small wins. It's never a good thing to ignore your people's successes, no matter what.

Often coaches will hide from problems. They think that by ignoring someone's poor performance either the employee or the performance will disappear.

You need to talk with them and try to repair what's broken. If you don't, it will only get worse. As a leader, you're not paid to ignore issues or people. Rather, you're role is to develop people so they can learn how to tackle problems for themselves and their team.

When a coach offers no response it disconnects behavior from reward. Further, when we inconsistently reward behaviors our employees don't know how to react.

So, no matter what the underlying truth or excuse is, consistent appropriate rewards are the key to positive reinforcement.

"I have been referred to as a disciplinarian, but I've never heard the word as pejorative. For me, a disciplinarian is someone who requires that people understand the consequences of their decisions."

- Coach Lou Holtz
Former University of Notre Dame football coach

Truth No. 6 – Their Attitude Reflects Your Leadership

I've found that the quickest and surest way to destroy excellence is not by rewarding it poorly or inconsistently, but rather by ignoring it completely.

I'm sure many of you, who have children, can relate to the following:

After a long day at work, you come home and finally get to sit in your most comfortable chair while drinking your favorite beverage. Then your child walks over and says, "Daddy, I drew you a picture."

You're not paying attention to little Johnny because you're watching the news or skimming the newspaper. He has drawn this beautiful picture with you in it. But you're so consumed with yourself, you ignore him.

Now Johnny returns later and says, "Daddy, I got a better picture this time. Look!" You ignore him again. How many times is Johnny going to come back to you with a picture? It's not going to happen too often. And that's the sad part. One day you're going to say, "I don't get pictures from you anymore. What's wrong with you Johnny? Why don't you draw me pictures anymore?"

And you're thinking, "Gee, Johnny doesn't have the same attitude he used to have. Johnny's behavior seems to have changed. What's wrong with him?" Nothing is wrong with Johnny. Something is wrong with you.

You need to respond. You need to decide what you want as a parent, a leader or a coach. What is the correct behavior?

Simply understand and commit to it and communicate it clearly and with consistent consequences. And then you need to consistently reward movement toward the goals you have set, even when you don't feel like it. Isn't that part of how you become a great parent? If we do what we want when we feel like it, we will not be effective parents. It's about doing the right thing at all times.

Player and employee neglect is not the way you coach to the goal when you're trying to make a positive difference.

Likewise, a critical response is also an inappropriate response. Little Johnny brings us a picture and we say, "Johnny, that picture is pretty good, but couldn't you have given Dad a little more hair? That picture is good, but isn't Dad taller than that? I'm not green. Why didn't you use a better color? And you didn't do it in the lines." What's going on here? Is it that Johnny doesn't get it? No.

We do not get it when we're critical, overly demanding and focused solely on the gap rather than talking about the good things they do. And he says, "Dad, I am 4." Johnny is saying to you that your expectations may be a little unreasonable.

We need to understand that negative responses are damaging. In Dale Carnegie's book, *How to Win Friends and Influence People*, he says never to criticize because it only causes people to become defensive. Then nothing constructive becomes of it. As a coach, our critical response to our players causes us to miss the goal. This negative response always misses the goal.

But, when we use failures to redirect and encourage, our players respond positively. As an individual they learn they have missed the mark, but they improve and the team moves forward.

> *"I'm in your corner. I believe in you."*
>
> **Said New York Yankee manager Joe Torre to former Yankee outfielder Paul O'Neill**

Michael Duke

Truth No. 7 – Be a Teacher

Basically, to grasp this response we must believe that our primary role as a coach is that of a teacher, regardless of what our job title implies.

- They call me the CEO, but I'm really a teacher.
- I'm a business owner, but I'm really a teacher.
- I'm a staff manager with a large corporation, but actually I'm a teacher.

When you think of a teacher, you probably picture someone standing at the front of a classroom instructing. However, all of us teach by our behaviors, our words and our attitudes.

We teach. And then we talk about what we're teaching. We're teaching what the right behavior is. That's why we've got to be involved. That's why we have to be aware of what's going on.

When we talk about this "redirect and encourage" response, the coach sets the standard. And when the employee doesn't meet the standard, the coach says, "Come over here and let's talk a little bit." "You know, I watched you and that's not the way we want that done. Let me show you how."

Can you see the Little League coach working with the child? "Now place your feet in the batter's box like so. And give me your hands. Hold the bat like this. Now when you swing, it should look like this." A coach doesn't just tell his player what to do. He patiently shows them over and over again. Why? Because he loves his players and he loves being a coach.

Do your people know what will happen to them if they miss an expectation? Many times we don't have in our handbook what the process is. I don't know why we don't. Let's just say the first time something happens we'll talk with you. We call that a verbal warning.

The second time you could have another verbal warning or you could have a written warning, but there's progressive discipline. It makes perfect sense for everybody to know what's going to happen. Just like a kid who knows that if he talks back to his mom, he's going to get time out. We know the infraction and we know what to expect. It's important that we know this so we don't have to guess.

Have you seen the movie *Remember the Titans*? How did the football team become victorious in the end? The coach understood the value of consequences. He set a higher standard for his players and held them accountable.

He was tough, a strict disciplinarian, but he established a relationship with each of them. It didn't matter if you were one of the star players or a player on the bench, there was always a built-in consequence.

Remember Coach Herman Boone's great speech in the movie about running a mile? His team knew that if they missed a block or a tackle, dropped a pass or fumbled they would run a mile. He demanded perfection of them in "every aspect of the game." And clear consequences made an impact and shaped performance. They became winners.

Do you have what it takes to be a coach? It's a tall order to care enough to set the standard, but it's even harder to follow through relentlessly.

Here's your takeaway. Coaches teach excellence or something else. What is the something else? Do you want the something else? Is there anything other than excellence that you want for your organization?

If you don't teach excellence, you're teaching something else. If you're not setting the bar high enough, you're not setting it in the direction toward excellence.

One of the most important things I'm going to say is that the ***consequence creates and clarifies the meaning of expectations.***

Let me give you an example. A memo comes out and the company is offering a new retirement benefit. One of those corporate deals. Everyone has to sign up to either accept or reject the benefit offering.

But George, in Information Technology, thinks this particular benefit is a waste of time. He does not want to fill out forms. George is too busy and doesn't see any value in it.

Everybody is filling out their forms, however. It's down to the wire now and the managers are talking about it. Everybody's forms are in but George's. Why? George's manager explains to his boss that George says he doesn't think it's important.

The general manager is now involved. He says, "Tell George he doesn't have to take the benefit. He just has to sign the form saying he rejects it. He doesn't see the importance of it," George's boss replies. "That is just what we told him," he added.

The General Manager finally says, "Tell George I need to see him." The manager sits down with George and says, "George you're a great IT guy, but there's a form that I need you to complete. Frankly, if you don't fill it out, I'm going to have to let you go."

George says, "Where's the form?" George signs the form and hands it back to his manager. "George, we've been trying to get you to sign this form for three months. Why did you sign it today?" the manager asks. "Nobody really explained it as clearly as you did," George replied.

Are you explaining it clearly? It's your job to give the right consequence to the right behavior. Remember, if you as a coach are not administering *appropriate consequences,* then the player will be less likely to deliver desired performance.

As a coach, you must do your job and do it well. If you're not willing or able to follow through with consequences, then they will not perform. They can't be great performers without you setting the standard and delivering the consequence.

This one single truth sets coaches apart from an ordinary business manager. They realize the power of the consequence!

You will not get proper performance if you're not giving an appropriate response. It's going to dwindle and subside. If you give negative responses, you'll get poor performance.

When you give the "redirect and encourage" response, you'll get improved performance. This response is a much better option.

Check it out. Think about the winningest coaches in your favorite sport. They had a program they enforced vigorously. What they expected of the players was clear and the cost for violating team rules was inescapable.

Recapping Truths 4-7 from Part Two:

4. **Earn the Right to Coach Everyday.** Who you are makes the difference. Calling yourself a coach does not make you one. You may know the game, but have you earned their trust and respect? Your challenge? To be worthy of the name "Coach."

5. **Clear, Consistent Accountability.** Do they know exactly what you expect from them and the price they will pay for not delivering? Your commitment to follow up and follow through creates winners.

6. **Their Attitude Reflects Your Leadership.** High-performing teams originate from high-performing coaches. Your lack of commitment, passion and determination will be apparent in their performance.

7. **Be a Teacher.** Never tell them what to do. Show them. Love the players and the game enough to teach them how to play it with passion and excellence. If you can't do this, you are in the wrong job.

Part Three: The Power of Praise

Truth No. 8 – No One Is There Yet

Now it's time to present you with the most significant consequence of all — praise.

"Praise is a consequence?" Indeed it is. And it's one consequence that people like.

Well-deserved praise will make a positive change in anyone's life. It feels good and I've seen many people go through a lot to hear personal praise again and again.

The key to effective praising is to praise progress constantly, whether people are finished with the project or not. What you don't want to communicate is, "You're not there yet." This will only dishearten them to learn and to do better.

None of us are perfect, yet too often we only want to praise perfection. What's important is that we praise significant progress along the way, not just the end result. Say, "Way to go, I'm seeing some progress."

It's like the Little League baseball player who gets his first hit. He steps up to home plate, hits the ball where no one can make a play, but dashes toward third base instead of first. The crowd chuckles, but because he has hit the ball for the first time, the coach lavishes him with praise. He's done his best. It was a big step in the right direction. Are we happy that he ran to third? No, but we can work on that while we praise the hit.

A lot of leaders hold back praise because "you're not there yet." Instead of saying, "You're not there yet," praise folks for things they have done well so far.

Praise helps cultivate progress. You might say, "Great job on the sale you made. I heard about how effectively you handled that issue." The greatest gift you can give anyone – whether it's one of your players on a ball team or a salesperson on your staff – is trust.

If you give people your trust, it will be reciprocated. The biggest problem you'll find is that you might have people who know what to do, but don't want to do it. I don't have a lot of patience for these folks, but I'll walk them through the incremental disciplinary process and terminate them if they continue to not want to perform. I want somebody in that slot who *wants* to do it right.

"I try to make every player on my team feel he's the spark keeping our machine in motion. On him depends our success."

- Coach Knute Rockne
Legendary University of Notre Dame football coach

Do you want anybody on your team, no matter how talented they are, who doesn't want to perform the best they can? This can infect your office, your team, your department and your company. So, you must set the tone and decide who stays and who goes.

Do you want someone who is giving half their heart on your ball club? Of course you don't. You want someone who will do a job big or small and do it well or not at all.

I'll take three Rudy's, who are on the bench cheering everybody else on, over a bunch of hot-shot players. Why? I want a team whose heart can be developed.

In Coach K's book, *Leading from the Heart,* he said: "Every year, my first priority is to find the heart of my team. The player who possessed superior passion and courage would become the core around which the entire team would be built."

It's so frustrating when people are working hard for you. They give you everything they got, and they get nothing in return.

I'll give you an example. I had worked for a guy and I had a really good year — one of those monumental career years. Sales grew from $6 million to more than $8 million. And my boss made a nice profit from my efforts.

We'd get these monthly reports that described current sales, last month's sales and last year's sales. It was clearly noted that I was up by as much as 40 percent in sales on the major product lines.

The report also said I was down by 5 percent to 10 percent on the few minor ones, which made up only 5 percent of our overall sales number.

My boss had only red marks all over the report, which stated I needed to work harder and do better on this part. "You need to focus on all these little things," he said. He didn't have one nice thing to say. I had to laugh. This is sad. I thought, "Why would I do what I do for him? I would do it for me, but surely not for him."

So as the employee, I confronted him and said, "Hey, why don't you put something nice on the report?" You know it wouldn't hurt, would it? I tried to teach him.

Why don't you put something other than a red mark on there? "Get a different color pen," I said in a teasing manner. He took it pretty well, but I was frustrated with the lack of balance and wanted to send him a message that it wouldn't hurt to say something nice. Do you do that?

People labor hard and all they get in return are red marks. They've put their heart and soul into a project and are deserving of praise.

It's not a motivator to see only red marks. Praise is so much better than that. To hear "this is such a beautiful piece of work" is a major motivator. You can guess the outcome. I stayed for a while but eventually left. The negativity was too much. I, like all people, want to be appreciated for a job well done.

In your mind you may say, "It's not perfect but for where you are, it's wonderful. It's extraordinary." You know it's not perfect, but that's not the point. You understand that it's significant progress.

In business, there is something called a Theory X and a Theory Y manager. Let's discuss the differences between them. Each have their own assumptions. Theory X managers assume people are lazy, incompetent and irresponsible.

You can imagine what kind of behaviors this provokes from employees, if you assume they're lazy, incompetent and irresponsible. These theories teach that people will rise or lower to the expectations placed on them.

As you read on, ask yourself which theory matches your leadership style best? Theory Y managers believe their people are creative, reliable and trustworthy. These are also assumptions.

The traditional approach matches up with the Theory X manager type. He or she tends to be top-down, authoritarian and centralized. "I've got to pay attention to my people because if I don't, they'll slack off."

"If it wasn't for me closely watching them and giving them good direction, there's just no telling what kind of work they would do." Is that hitting a little to close to home for anybody? The need to control. The need to direct. The need to be the one who can say, "They're doing good work because they're doing what I told them. They're following my orders. They're following my lead."

In that model, you don't value your employees. Plus, you as the leader see yourself as the one who makes it happen. You see yourself as the important one. Your people aren't important – you are.

We're going to talk in a minute about the acorn philosophy. But the other philosophy that some people have is called the "empty vessel." My people are "empty vessels." I'm going to give them what they need. All they need is what I give them. I don't want anybody else to give anything to them. Doesn't this remind you of a Theory X manager?

They're empty, except for what I tell them. This is so arrogant. It's rather silly to think that you're going to be the one who is everything and that they don't bring anything to the table.

The "acorn approach" is very different from the "empty vessel" approach. You can imagine how people respond to this one. This approach says, "I trust my people. I'm going to get them involved."

Power flows up through the ranks. Who really knows how to do a job well except for the people doing the job? I'm going to empower them.

Perhaps most important, I'm going to trust them to do the right thing and tell them to come to me. If you need something from me, you can come to me and I'll do my best to get it for you.

The quality of your responses as a leader affects the quality of responses from your people. Do you see that?

If you're controlling and directing, there are some great people who will find that stifling. Just turn me loose and let me go, rather than hovering so much.

Remember that Lombardi was able to come in and interact with those men and turn them into winners. Amazingly, Lombardi very seldom called the plays from the sidelines. That blew me away to learn that. He was such a disciplinarian.

In fact, he made sure that everyone was prepared during practices. On game day, he'd call a half a dozen plays and trusted his quarterback to call the rest.

That's the way it was. He was relentless in preparation. And he set incredibly high standards when it came to getting the job done right. Yet when it came to game day he turned his players loose.

Trust your people to do the job right. Empower them and turn them loose. You can discourage your people with your own controlling management approach. The one that says, "I don't trust you to do it right."

It's like when you walk in a 7-Eleven convenience store and ask the attendant for the key to the restroom. The attendant gives you the key, but it has a two-foot long stick attached to it so you don't steal it. I promise that I don't want to steal your key, but now you've made me feel like a thief.

Let me tell you a story. The publishing company I had worked for had a manager who believed in controlling the budget. The sales people would turn in their advertising at the end of the day. You'd fill out various forms and there was a table where all the sales people would gather in order to complete their paperwork.

There were pens and tape dispensers, all of which were chained to the table. And if you needed another pen or more tape, all the supplies were in the general manager's office. You had to come in and say, "Mr. Jones, I need a pen." And he would say, "What happened to your other pen?" And do you know what the people did? They purchased their own pens, tape dispensers and tape.

So, all over the office, everyone had their very own tape dispensers with their name on it. They protected them like gold. They hoarded them and would not share.

People aren't motivated in a situation like that. They react to the way they are treated. If you withhold trust from people, they will behave in untrustworthy ways.

An acorn, however, is interesting. It's very small. And after you plant it into the ground, a beautiful and magnificent Oak tree grows from it. I had a large Oak tree in my backyard, which had leaves of splendid colors. You couldn't reach your arms half way around it.

Compare the acorn approach to the empty vessel approach. What kind of response are you going to get if everyone knows you believe they are acorns, which have the capability of becoming mighty Oaks?

Let me go back and tie these two together now. One of the things you're doing, and perhaps don't realize, is that it can be very positive when you issue consequences to people when you challenge them to do better.

Your approach matters. It will have a lot to do with whether your people respond and become winners. Lombardi turned 13 NFL players into All Pros. Are you turning your people into winners? Or, are you frustrating them?

These are the questions you need to ask yourself. You can frustrate with neglect or criticism. But with redirection and encouragement, you can make a vast difference in someone's life and career.

You might say to a player, "Your attitude is not where it needs to be. It needs to improve. Your performance, which is average, is not to your standards. You can do better." People say that's a criticism. But at its heart, many achievers will hear that as a compliment. If said with love and conviction, these few words, "*You can do better*," can make a world of difference!

You know what? They expect more of me. That must mean they think I can do more. We want to deliver and we want to step up. If you reward your kids and you say you were an F student, but now you are a D student, you give them a small reward. Then they move to a C student and you increase the reward to something greater.

Now they are a C student and perhaps that's the best they can be. But that's not enough. There's got to be something there that says you're making progress, but you've got more. I know there's more in you. We're going to reward you for the next step. It may be a C-plus or B-minus. But you know what? We're going to find where that next step is. We are going to take you as far as you'll let me take you.

Believing in people. Isn't that big? And often all it takes is a few encouraging words. You *can* do this!

"Treat people as if they were what they ought to be and you will help them become what they are capable of being."

- Johann Wolfgang Goethe
German poet and philosopher

Michael Duke

Truth No. 9 – Love Them or Trade Them

There are times when people who were once great are not any longer. These situations can be difficult and stressful for the coach. When you decide that somebody on your team, somebody who's on your bus seat can't perform anymore, then it's time to put somebody else in that seat.

Because when you stop loving them. When you lose faith in them and are no longer committed, your employees will sense it.

There's a successful leader and entrepreneur in town – a true gentleman. In his industry, he's a legend in Kentucky. I worked with his organization while providing leadership training. As I was working with their leaders, I asked them: "When was the last time somebody was fired here?" They all looked around and laughed while replying, "Never!" I asked, "What happened?" "Surely there have been people who've come in and not performed well."

You know what he did when people did not meet his expectations over time? "He just ignores you." "He just won't return your calls."

Then people will get frustrated and leave. That's what the good people do. The excellent people that think highly of themselves will not put up with that. But the people who are complacent will put up with it. This sounds like an extreme case and it is, but leaders are ignoring their people and their roles.

When you as a coach don't do your job well, the talented and committed people leave first because they want to be treated with respect and dignity. They want to excel and be appreciated. Again, the greatest gift you can give is trust. Trust is the fuel every organization needs.

Michael Duke

> *"Trust men and they will be true to you; treat them greatly and they will show themselves to be great."*
>
> **- Ralph Waldo Emerson**
> **19th Century writer and public speaker**

You've got to put it out there. I believe you are great. I believe you have the potential for greatness. Therefore, I'm expecting great things from you.

Why are you so tough on me? When I missed that sale you didn't let me off the hook. You challenged me. Yes I did. You can do better. I expect you to do better.

You frustrate people when you challenge them to step beyond their capabilities. Just like little kids. But it's the coach's job to find each player's optimal level of performance and then continue to gradually raise the bar. This represents the level of excellence they can achieve whenever their best is required of them — whether its sports, business or life in general.

Imagine Johnny up there swinging the bat as he keeps missing the ball. The coach is screaming, "Johnny you're killing me." "What am I going to do with you Johnny?" Now Johnny wants to quit.

He wants to quit, but he needs support if he's going to mature into a mighty Oak. We've got to understand the need to give before we can get. All positive behaviors must be rewarded immediately.

The coach says to the player, "Way to go! Good swing!" The coach says to the employee, "That's exactly what I'm looking for. That attitude you demonstrated with the customer who was yelling and screaming at you was perfect. You showed patience and understanding. The way you handled the objection, as well as the way you dealt with your subordinate was also perfect. I saw it. I heard it. Way to go!" Coaches know how to do that.

Be specific about what they did right or almost right. It's not about being there yet. Rather, it's that you're making great progress. Make that be your overriding compliment. "You're making progress." Compared to where you were a month ago or three months ago, you're light years ahead.

They know they are not where they are supposed to be, but you can praise the movement. By doing so, you encourage continued progress in the right direction.

Michael Duke

Truth No. 10 – Treat Them As if They Were "More Than"

Share your positive feelings about what they did. This is where people get uncomfortable, most of whom are men struggling to express themselves. But it's important to speak from your heart and say, "I am proud of you. It really touches me that you would give the extra effort like you did. I just want to tell you that it really means a lot. From my heart, thank you. Thank you for your contribution."

The employee can't believe it. Man, wow! The way he looked at me. He had a tear in his eye, as he said it. You think about that. And you reflect for a while. And you're saying, "This is cool." I felt it. He really does appreciate my contribution.

The greatest retention strategy in the world is this right here. It's not money, just be competitive in your market. ***The greatest retention strategy in the world is your love and respect.***

If you're the coach, the leader or the manager and you love and respect your employees, it will work out. Your retention will skyrocket. Share your positive feelings. Encourage them to keep up the good work.

What if you have employees that are poor performers? Do you see some of your people as less than? This is real-world stuff. I often hear this from my clients. "Michael, I want to praise my people, but quite frankly they don't deserve it. I want to give them a pat on the back, although they foul up as soon as I do. It seems so inconsistent. So how do I handle that?"

Let's talk about this. If you see your people as less than, you've already made that decision. They're not going to cut it. If you treat your people as less than, they'll act and perform at your "less than" expectations.

You've heard those terrible stories about parents telling their kids, "You're nothing. And you will never amount to anything." What do you think they're going to grow up to be? More than likely, nothing or at least "less than."

Some break away from their parents' vision and say, "I don't care what you say; I'm going to be what is important to me." I tell you the gravitational pull against that is strong.

However, we all subtly do this with our people. We've got to ask ourselves, "Are we communicating to our people that they are less than or more than?" I believe you can be more than and I expect more from you.

This is encouraging if it communicates that the person, the coach believes in you.

The power of praise is in the prophecy. You're casting a vision for them in their life. And you know what they're going to do. As the son is to the father, or the player is to the coach, or the worker is to the boss, they'll fulfill your dream for them. They want to do that for you. They want to make you proud.

Coach to the Goal

I have always enjoyed watching my boys play baseball. When I think of how a single event can positively impact a life, I recall a beautiful summer day. . . . It was a day I will never forget. I was sitting in the stands at the time, right behind home plate.

My son, Alex, was playing in a machine-pitch baseball game and was a 6-year-old at the time. He was on the pitcher's mound waiting to field ground balls as they were hit. Most of the hit balls at this level of play rarely left the infield.

But a player got up there to bat and "WHAP!" It was a line shot, which was headed at Alex. You should have seen the look on his face. He reacted so quickly, raising his glove as much to shield his face from the ball as to catch it. And when he looked into his mitt, he got the surprise of his life – the ball!

Michael Duke

Everybody was cheering and screaming. It was one of those special moments. People were there to share it and it lasted for days. We spoke of it often. What a catch! Wasn't that awesome? Alex would say, "Can you believe it Dad? I can't believe I really caught it," he exclaimed. I said, "Yes, I believe it son. You are an awesome baseball player!"

But if a few days later I had asked him, "When are you going to do that again? Or had said, "Yeah you did that once, but it's been a while." That would have been a wet blanket to the sweet moment he had recently enjoyed.

We must learn to savor our successes and the successes of our team. Savor them and let them linger. That's one thing I encourage my clients to do: Celebrate more. Spontaneous celebration. Not just big parties that cost a lot of money. Just celebrate.

David Novak with Yum! Brands, Inc. gives extra performers rubber chickens. What do you think they cost at a gag store? About $1.87 for a goofy, little rubber chicken. But his people love to receive a rubber chicken from Mr. Novak.

You need to give people a rubber chicken or whatever. Give them something they want. They'll try to meet expectations because they want positive consequences.

"We treat people like royalty. If you honor and serve people who work for you, they will honor and serve you."

- Mary Kay Ash
Founder of Mary Kay Cosmetics

But some of you are going to say, "I want to praise my people, although I have people who are truly not what they ought to be. They're less than." Well, here's your answer: Own it. They are yours. You hired them. Deal with it.

Tell them what you expect. Help them understand what the expectation is. Let them put a plan together so that they can meet those expectations. Give them 60 to 90 days. And if they can't do it, love them.

Throw a party for them and move them out. Tell them, "Thank you for your contribution. We appreciate everything you've done and we hope that you provide as much value or more to your next employer as you've given us.

In the world of professional sports, we call this trading up. It's your responsibility to bring quality people in. All great coaches take their role as recruiter very seriously. And it's also your responsibility if they can't meet expectations. Once you've done everything you can for them, move them out.

You have got to own it. And shame on every manager that says, "It's not my fault. It's my employee's fault that my department is not meeting expectations."

We've got to step up and say it's mine. It's my team. I'm the leader and the coach. I'm the one who makes it happen, and we've got to make it happen through these players. Maybe you, the coach, need to grow.

Maybe you need some different players. You've got to look at each case individually. But great coaches never blame their people. Never!

They don't say, "I had such a great plan this year, but my quarterback stunk and my running back kept fumbling." What kind of relationship are you going to build with your players if you're constantly blaming them for the team's failures?

Every great coach says, "You know, I should have done a better job (better Coach Preparation). I should have led them better (again Coach Preparation).

I should have anticipated some things. We're going to learn, grow and get better."

Each failure is an opportunity to learn. And that's important to ingrain, especially when it comes to a winner. The sad thing is that you get great people and now the managers are not dealing with an issue and the great player on the team feels disrespected and they leave.

They have been there for 5, 10, 15 or 20 years. They were an incredible performer and now that they leave, everybody bad mouths them. Now after leaving, they weren't that good because management is trying to justify to themselves why the employee left.

This should never happen. We should ask, "What could we have done differently to keep the person here?" "What can I do next time so a player of that caliber doesn't leave?" I want to keep all the great ones. I want to keep all the average ones so that they can become great one day.

In summary, the leader sets the context. You're the gardener. You're tilling the garden. You're planting the seeds so that the rain and the sunshine can make them grow. You're going to keep out the obstacles and create a nurturing environment.

Now they have to bring heart and will. But you're creating an environment of accountability. Remember what Coach Boone said, "When you put on this uniform, you will be excellent." So when they step up, you need to make sure that the direction is excellence. Confidence is so critical.

You have an incredibly influential role on your people when it comes to their confidence. If you believe in them, they're much more likely to believe in themselves.

Again, think about the little league kids. Johnny is up there to bat, he's had 10 at-bats. He's swinging and he is not even close to hitting the ball. He's up there whiffing away and the coach is saying, "That's alright."

That's what everybody does when they start. Baseball legend Mickey Mantle missed the ball a lot. Even Mark McGwire and Sammy Sosa struck out a lot early in their careers. That's OK.

If you keep swinging, you'll begin to hit the ball. Think about that truth. If you keep trying, you'll eventually hit the ball. And they come back after making their first hit and say, "You were right coach. I didn't give up. I kept trying and I hit the ball."

Now they believe in you and they have confidence in themselves because what you said was true. That's what we do with our children. It's what we do with our people. It's what coaches do with their team!

You've got to have confidence in them. And it's just like in Parliaments when we have a "no confidence" vote. Right? The leader goes! We've lost our confidence in the coach. And sometimes the coach should go instead of the players.

But everything you say, your behavior, your demeanor, your example sets the tone for what you believe. So many times you don't have to say things. It's your life and your actions.

And your greatest calling as a coach is to believe in the people around you. To see the greatness that's inside them. This is true.

Think about your child who is struggling in school or with social relationships. You're there to encourage them, but not to enable them. You're there to say: "Hey, keep trying. Never stop trying. Keep going. It's going to be OK. Take risks. And I'll be here if you fail. But the only way for you to succeed is to keep trying."

And the kid understands, and one day develops self-confidence, but the parent had the confidence in the child first. As a leader or manager, believe in your people. And if you believe in your people, they'll be able to one day believe in themselves. But so many times, learners cop an attitude. And someone cops an attitude with them, and they get frustrated. They don't get it.

They get this negativity, which is an obstacle to their development.

The coach's faith in the individual is one day transferred. Think about the teacher who had challenged you. Think about the coaches who've made a positive difference in your life because they had fostered your self-confidence.

Coaches teach truth. We talk about being a teacher. What do we teach? We teach truth. We teach excellence. Lombardi looked at those players in 1960, when he took over and said, "I know what you look like, but that's not who you are."

Now think about the things he might have said. "If you do what I say and if you follow my program, you'll be winners. You need to believe in me. And if you trust me, you'll not be sorry. I'll turn you into winners."

You think he said something like that? They started winning, and then things changed and they became winners.

This is from an article out of *The Courier-Journal* newspaper in Louisville, Kentucky. This is Rick Pitino's first year in Louisville. Ellis Myles had an attitude problem before Pitino took over, but Myles said:

"At first I thought he was like every other coach, just trying to get on me, to give me a hard time, to get me to do what they wanted. But I started to understand that if I do what Coach Pitino is trying to teach me to do, I'll be a better player and I'll be more successful when basketball is over."

That's what great coaches do. Listen, I have something important to teach you. And when you don't meet my expectation, then you're going to run a mile. But when you do, I'm going to love on you. I'm going to love on you like nobody's loved on you since your mother. Right? But I'm also going to ding you when you have it coming. You're going to always know where you stand with me. Isn't that what coaches do? But if you listen to me, then I'll make you a winner.

Recapping Truths 8-10 from Part Three:

8. **No One Is There Yet.** Your constant criticism is destructive. If you want winners then change your perspective. Praise incremental progress to the goal. Then stand back and watch them win!

9. **Love Them or Trade Them.** When you stop believing that they can do the job, they can feel it. Do them a favor. Give them opportunity to be a winner elsewhere. Use this as a chance to learn from your own mistakes and upgrade the position.

10. **Treat Them As if They Were "More Than."** Your genuine, heartfelt confidence in their ability makes excellence possible. Cast an inspiring vision for each player on your team. Give them something to reach for and live up to.

Conclusion

The *Coach to the Goal* leadership philosophy is about helping others become winners. I cannot think of a nobler goal. Great coaches understand that people need a safe, supportive environment in which to thrive. People learn best and will extend themselves when they know they are respected and loved for who they are. If you have been guilty of diminishing this relational component in your leadership style, you will forever limit your team's potential to perform.

When you – as their leader and coach – have earned their respect, loyalty and love, only then will they begin to become all that their gifts and talents have fully equipped them to be.

But here is the hard reality. Most coaches fall short on the two extremes of the leadership continuum. In trying to be nurturing and supportive, they become soft and wishy-washy. In trying to be strong and decisive, they become harsh, negative and overly demanding. None of these undesirable qualities are to be confused with having a genuine respect for all people along with clear, tough accountability for excellence and a strong well-defined culture that reflects these values.

A great coach, who coaches to the goal, grasps this need for balance. They are the first to praise. They attentively listen and appropriately respond. They use failure as teaching opportunities in order to develop the person and move the organization forward. The coach cares for their people from the heart, but this does not mean they accept anything less than their best attitude and effort.

They are ruthlessly consistent in maintaining high standards. Plus, they meet clear and appropriate consequences without apology. There are no surprises, no favoritism and no confusion. The coach has moved everyone to the same page.

People respond to a coach who understands the goal. They respond with respect, loyalty and a tremendous desire to please. Performance improves as respect increases, and the player begins to believe they are developing personally and professionally.

As this realization deepens, it dawns on the player that if they listen, learn and follow the coach, then one day they may become great!

I believe in the power of great coaches to transform lives. I am convinced that if you apply the 10 truths within the pages of this book, you will positively impact the lives of the people who matter most to you. These people may be employees, team members, children or players on your team.

As you live and teach others to *Coach to the Goal,* you enjoy the true reward of leadership – you get to see your people win! Better yet, you get to teach them what winning really means.

Winning has never been about the final score, but rather about the journey. As the incomparable Coach John Wooden said, "You are to be able to perform at your best when your best is required." This commitment to excellence may be learned in sports or at work, but it can and should be applied to every aspect of our lives.

I wish you every success. And may your dedication and passion for coaching bring you rich rewards, as you touch others and help them become all that God intended them to be.

Thank you from my heart for sharing my passion with me. Now go "coach to the goal!"

Acknowledgements

I am honored by your interest in *Coach to the Goal*. My prayer is that all of you have been challenged and filled. For sharing this joy with me, I say "thank you." For allowing me to do what I love, I respond with a full heart. God bless you all. Special thanks go to Laura Duke. A project of this magnitude requires hours of sacrifice. She has endured my passion graciously.

I also want to thank Ray Strothman, founder and managing partner of Strothman & Company. Ray, you were my first client and your team was the first to hear *Coach to the Goal* in a seminar format in 2003. And to my dear friends Glenn Bednarczyq, David Jarnagin, Bill Meyer, David Stewart and David Watson, your loyalty and support mean more than you will ever know. You guys have been my biggest cheerleaders.

Jeff Emerson, my Editorial Advisor, has made this work come to life. Jeff, *Coach to the Goal,* would not exist without you. And to Todd Engel who designed the cover, which captured what the book is all about. Thank you!

I have borrowed heavily from the works of others in this presentation. Truths from the teachings of Jesus Christ will be evident and I hope will reflect the glory due Him.

My coaching philosophy has been impacted largely because of Ken Blanchard's writings. He offers remarkable insight into a truly people-based management system. To those of you who are familiar with his books, *The One Minute Manager*, *Putting the One Minute Manager to Work* and *Whale Done*, the impact of his work on this project is apparent.

Recommended Reading on the Subject of Coaching

1. *Coaching for Teamwork* by Vince Lombardi Jr.

2. *What it takes to be #1* by Vince Lombardi Jr.

3. *Everyone's a Coach* by Ken Blanchard and Don Shula.

4. *Leading with the Heart* by Mike Krzyzewski.

5. *Wooden on Leadership* by John Wooden and Steve Jamison.

6. *Winning Everyday* by Lou Holtz.

7. *Joe Torre's Ground Rules for Winners* by Joe Torre.

8. *When Pride Still Mattered, A Life of Vince Lombardi* by David Maraniss.

9. *The One Minute Manager* by Ken Blanchard Ph. D. and Spencer Johnson M. D.

10. *Putting the One Minute Manager to Work* by Ken Blanchard Ph. D. and Robert Lorber M.D.

11. *Whale Done* by Ken Blanchard Ph. D., Thad Lucinak, Chuck Tompkins and Jim Ballard.

The following list has been compiled to challenge the truly hungry and curious. It is composed of books that have profoundly influenced Michael's thinking and therefore his personal and management philosophy.

Michael's Top 10

1. *The Bible* by God. If you have not read this, you are truly missing out. It is far more than a book of rules to make you feel guilty. It is food for your soul.

2. *The One Minute Manager* by Ken Blanchard and Spencer Johnson M.D. It is simple yet profound. You are never too young or too old to learn to put people first in business.

3. *The Seven Habits of Highly Effective People* by Stephen Covey. These are enduring principles to live by for spiritual and organizational growth.

4. *Wild at Heart* by John Eldredge. I read the pages and was blown away. It is one of the few books I have read and reread several times. No other book has spoken to me in such a

personal way. John asks the questions I have asked for years and also provides some interesting and challenging answers.

5. *Waking the Dead* by John Eldredge. If you have an interest in the spiritual, this book will open your eyes. His approach is truly unique. He will help you see this world as you never have before.

6. *Good to Great* by James C. Collins and Jerry I. Porras. Every business owner, every business man or woman needs to devour this book. It is rock solid and one of the most practical guides to organizational success to date.

7. *Love is the Killer App* by Tim Sanders. Tim has it down. Share. Give it away. And I mean the good stuff. This book spoke truth to me in a way that few have. Share your knowledge. Share your network. Share your love. And it all will come back to you…and more!

8. *The Goal* by Eliyahu M. Goldratt and Jeff Cox. Is it a management text or a novel? Is it a about business challenges or the trials of living successfully in your personal life. This author

speaks truth. He was the first secular writer to make it plain to me that if something is true, then it is true all the time regardless of context.

9. *Love* by Leo Buscaglia. The world needs love. We need to talk about it, live it and express it. Leo Buscaglia makes you want to do just that.

10. *Boundaries* by Henry Cloud M.D. and John Townsend M.D. This book opened my eyes to the significance and complexities of human relationships. They offer principles that simplify and clarify something that so many of us see as so vague and challenging. I have quoted this book as much or more as any I have read.

About the Author

Michael Duke has led a remarkably diversified life. He has been in the ministry, sales, corporate management and most recently an entrepreneur. Michael Duke is not only a gifted communicator; he truly understands people, which is why Michael is so successful at getting to the heart of so many issues. It may have been Michael's brief career in the ministry, which has served as an important foundation for his success in motivating and managing people.

Michael began his sales and marketing career 20 years ago with Curtis Industries, a national hardware company, where he ranked in the top 10 of 250 sales associates and was accepted in the prestigious Presidents Inner Circle. At age 26, Michael became the youngest district manager in the country.

He has also enjoyed a distinguished management career with *Auto Trader* magazine in which he orchestrated a successful turnaround and facilitated an acquisition of a primary competitor. While accomplishing this phenomenal success in his career, Michael earned a graduate degree in Management in 1986.

Michael soon discovered that he had the heart of a teacher and began a parallel career as a college instructor. As a natural outgrowth of his love for teaching and helping others, Michael established his consulting business in 2000 and now devotes his full schedule consulting and speaking to businesses in the region.

Many can personally attest that Michael's passion is people. He is a motivator and problem solver. Some refer to Michael as "Louisville's best business teacher." But his clients simply refer to him as "trusted friend and advisor."

Share It with Others

To order single copies of *Coach to the Goal: 10 Truths to Transform Your Team into Winners,* simply

Call **Harrods Creek Publishing** at **(502) 253-0899**

or

Visit Michael Duke online at **www.michaelduke.com**

Coach to the Goal: 10 Truths to Transform Your Team into Winners and other books by Harrods Creek Publishing are available at special quantity discounts for bulk purchases for sales promotions, premiums, fund-raising or educational use. Special books or book excerpts also can be created to fit individual needs.

For details about bulk quantity purchases and more information, call Harrods Creek Publishing at **(502) 253-0899** or write to:

Harrods Creek Publishing
P.O. Box 43784
Louisville, Kentucky 40258

How to Invite Michael to Speak

If you would like Michael to come and share the 10 truths of the *Coach to the Goal* message with your team, call 502-**253-0899** or visit **www. michaelduke.com.**

You will find him engaging and passionate about making a positive difference in the lives of the people who matter most to you.

www.ingramcontent.com/pod-product-compliance
Lightning Source LLC
Chambersburg PA
CBHW030839180526
45163CB00004B/1377